Faith Comes From Hearing

I0559460

PUBLISHED by PARABLES

Earthly Stories with a Heavenly Meaning

Faith Comes From Hearing

Faith Comes From Hearing
Dolores Jackson

PUBLISHED by PARABLES
Earthly Stories with a Heavenly Meaning

Faith Comes From Hearing
Dolores Jackson

Published By Parables
April, 2024

Printed in the United States of America

Readers should be aware that Internet Web sites offered as citations and/or sources for further information may have been changed or disappeared between the time this was written and the time it is read.

Faith Comes From Hearing

Dolores Jackson

PUBLISHED *by* PARABLES
Earthly Stories with a Heavenly Meaning

Dolores Jackson

Presented to

_____

By

_____

On the Occasion of

_____

Date

_____

Dedication

This book is dedicated to the following:

First, I thank the tireless efforts of Dr. John Dee Jeffries, Samantha Fury and "Published **by Parables**", who believed in this project from the beginning, and their dedicated team: Your unwavering commitment to quality and excellence made this book possible.

To my beloved sons, **David Stroud and James Phillips**, your unwavering support and encouragement have been my pillars of strength. Your belief in me inspires me to pursue my calling wholeheartedly.

And to all my **Precious Prayer Partners**, your steadfast prayers, unwavering faith, and boundless love have illuminated my path as I follow God's will for my life.

I sincerely thank each of you for serving as my steadfast guides and companions throughout this remarkable journey of faith in Jesus Christ.

Faith Comes From Hearing Activating Your Spiritual Journey

Introduction

I believe God inspires this book and that it is not a coincidence that you are reading these words right now. God is intentional, and nothing He does is by happenstance because everything He does is by divine design. With purpose, He will accomplish His will in your life.

You may be wondering why a Good God, a loving God, would allow you to go through such painful trials. God is taking us all to a place of complete reliance and faith in Him. He has promised that He will never leave you or forsake you, that when we go through deep waters, God says, "I will be with you... when you go through the fire, you will not be burned..."

Why Do We Find It So Hard to Trust Him? The Bible does not say that we will not have difficulties but rather the opposite, that we will have tribulations, but Jesus said, "Fear not for I have overcome the world."

He died for the whole world, which means You. The veil was torn from the top to the bottom, allowing us direct access to our Heavenly Father. No longer separated by sin, we now have full access to God, who is Holy.

I pray that this book will cause your faith and prayer life to grow exponentially and that you have a "working knowledge" of God's word and how it applies to your life and well-being. May the Lord God bless you, cause His face to shine upon you, and give you His peace.

Waiting on The Lord

Let's pause for a moment and explore the meaning of wait. What does it really entail? Webster's Dictionary offers some clues: "To stay or rest in expectation; to stop or remain stationary, till the arrival of some person or event." Waiting is not a passive state but an active one. It is holding on to hope and trusting God's promises. It is knowing that He listens to our prayers and responds in His perfect timing. Waiting can test our patience and faith, especially when we feel like God is silent or distant. But we should never doubt His love and care for us. He is always there with us to guide, comfort, provide, and empower us as we wait for His will to unfold.

Philippians 4:6-7 AMP

[6] Do not be anxious or worried about anything, but in everything [every circumstance and situation] by prayer and petition with thanksgiving, continue to make your [specific] requests known to God. [7] And the peace of God [that peace which reassures the heart, that peace] which transcends all understanding, [that peace which] stands guard over your hearts and your minds in Christ Jesus [is yours].

Hebrews 11:3 AMP

[3] By faith [that is, with an inherent trust and enduring confidence in the power, wisdom and goodness of God] we understand that the worlds (universe, ages) were framed and created [formed, put in order, and equipped for their intended purpose] by the word of God, so that what is seen was not made out of things which are visible.

Hebrews 11:6 AMP

[6] But without faith it is impossible to [walk with God and] please Him, for whoever comes [near] to God must [necessarily] believe that God exists and that He rewards those who [earnestly and diligently] seek Him.

Matthew 21:21-22 AMP

[21] Jesus replied to them, "I assure you and most solemnly say to you, if you have faith [personal trust and confidence in Me] and do not doubt or allow yourself to be drawn in two directions, you will not only do what was done to the fig tree, but even if you say to this mountain, 'Be taken up and thrown into the sea,' it will happen [if God wills it]. [22] And whatever you ask for in prayer, believing, you will receive."

Matthew 7:7-11 AMP

[7] "Ask and keep on asking and it will be given to you; seek and keep on seeking and you will find; knock and keep on knocking and the door will be opened to you. [8] For everyone who keeps on asking receives, and he who keeps on seeking finds, and to him who keeps on knocking, it will be opened. [9] Or what man is there among you who, if his son asks for bread, will [instead] give him a stone? [10] Or if he asks for a fish, will [instead] give him a snake? [11] If you then, evil (sinful by nature) as you are, know how to give good and advantageous gifts to your children, how much more will your Father who is in heaven [perfect as He is] give what is good and helpful to those who keep on asking Him.

Psalm 27:14 AMP

[14] Wait for and confidently expect the LORD; Be strong and let your heart take courage; Yes, wait for and confidently expect the LORD.

Psalm 130:5 AMP

[5] I wait [patiently] for the LORD, my soul [expectantly] waits, And in His word do I hope.

Proverbs 3:5-8 ESV

[5] Trust in the LORD with all your heart, and do not lean on your own understanding. [6] In all your ways acknowledge him, and he will make straight your paths. [7] Be not wise in your own eyes; fear the LORD, and turn away from evil. [8] It will be healing to your flesh and refreshment to your bones.

Prayer

Heavenly Father, It's not always easy to trust Your timing through suffering, illnesses, and uncertainty, but Your word says in Psalm 27:14, "Wait on the Lord: Be of good courage, and He shall strengthen thine heart: wait, I say on the Lord." Strengthen me now, Lord, and help me to be of good courage as I wait to see the salvation of the Lord. Amen

As Believers, desiring God's will for our lives should be a fundamental aspect of our faith. Regardless of what we pray for or about, our underlying motivation should always be, "If it is God's will." Sometimes, we do not receive the answers we hoped for from the Lord, and we wonder why.

In such moments, it is essential to pause, re-examine our desires, and surrender our will to God; in doing so, we then release the situation to the Lord in total surrender.

The hymn "I SurrenderAll" beautifully captures this spirit of yielding to God's plan. If you have not already, I encourage you to explore the story behind this timeless song. Desiring God's will can be challenging; it's one thing to pray about getting a job, but what about when we are praying for a loved one to be healed from some catastrophic illness? Letting go of a loved one who is at or near the end of life can be heartbreaking and devastating. Do you trust God enough to let His will be done in your life? If yes, then we can't expect to always know what's best in every situation.

Matthew 26:36-38 ESV

[36] Then Jesus went with them to a place called Gethsemane, and he said to his disciples, "Sit here, while I go over there and pray." [37] And taking with him Peter and the two sons of Zebedee, he began to be sorrowful and troubled. [38] Then he said to them, "My soul is very sorrowful, even to death; remain here, and watch with me."

Matthew 6:9-10 ESV

[9] Pray then like this: "Our Father in heaven, hallowed be your name. [10] Your kingdom come, your will be done, on earth as it is in heaven.

God's Plan for You

Many Christians today want to find God's plan for their life but, sadly, they often overlook the one place where God's plan for our lives is revealed—the Bible. His overall goal for each of us is that we would bring Him glory, and He uses both His Spirit and Word to accomplish this.

Jeremiah 29:11 AMP

"For I know the plans and thoughts that I have for you,' says the LORD, 'plans for peace and well-being and not for disaster to give you a future and a hope."

Jeremiah 1:5 ESV

"Before I formed you in the womb I knew you, and before you were born I consecrated you; I appointed you a prophet to the nations."

Psalm 139:13-14 ESV

"For you formed my inward parts; you knitted me together in my mother's womb. I praise you, for I am fearfully and wonderfully made. Wonderful are your works; my soul knows it very well."

Psalm 139:16-18 ESV

Your eyes saw my unformed substance; in your book were written, every one of them, the days that were formed for me, when as yet there was none of them. How precious to me are your thoughts, O God! How vast is the sum of them! If I would count them, they are more than the sand. I awake, and I am still with you.

Ephesians 1:3-6 ESV

[3] Blessed be the God and Father of our Lord Jesus Christ, who has blessed us in Christ with every spiritual blessing in the heavenly places, [4] even as he chose us in him before the foundation of the world, that we should be holy and blameless before him. In love [5] he predestined us for adoption to himself as sons through Jesus Christ, according to the purpose of his will, [6] to the praise of his glorious grace, with which he has blessed us in the Beloved.

Reflection

Have you discerned God's divine calling upon your life? Are you aware of the spiritual endowments and innate abilities bestowed upon you by the Creator?

I earnestly implore you to embark on a journey of self-discovery, to unearth the distinctive capabilities entrusted to you by the Almighty. In this pursuit, I encourage you to seek divine counsel through prayer, asking the Lord to illuminate the path He desires for you to tread with your gifts and talents.

Prayer

Heavenly Father, Your thoughts of me are more than the sand on the seashore; You created me and knitted me together in my mother's bomb; You know my thoughts from afar off, and my days You had numbered before there was even one. You, O'Lord, are the great I Am, Almighty, All-Knowing; I trust Your plan. Amen

Faith Comes From Hearing

Spiritual Gifts

Each believer receives at least one gift.

1 Corinthians 12:4-11 ESV

[4] Now there are varieties of gifts, but the same Spirit; [5] and there are varieties of service, but the same Lord; [6] and there are varieties of activities, but it is the same God who empowers them all in everyone. [7] To each is given the manifestation of the Spirit for the common good. [8] For to one is given through the Spirit the utterance of wisdom, and to another the utterance of knowledge according to the same Spirit, [9] to another faith by the same Spirit, to another gifts of healing by the one Spirit, [10] to another the working of miracles, to another prophecy, to another the ability to distinguish between spirits, to another various kinds of tongues, to another the interpretation of tongues. [11] All these are empowered by

one and the same Spirit, who apportions to each one individually as he wills.

The Holy Spirit determines who receives which gifts.

1 Corinthians 12:7 ESV

[7] To each is given the manifestation of the Spirit for the common good.

1 Corinthians 12:11 ESV

[11] All these are empowered by one and the same Spirit, who apportions to each one individually as he wills.

Prayer

Heavenly Father, Help me use the spiritual gifts You have blessed me with to bring You glory and edify the Church. Father, I pray that You will give me a fresh anointing for every new challenge, equipping me to minister in power, love, and wisdom.

We are to use our gifts to serve others, benefiting the body of Christ (the Church).

1 Corinthians 12:21-26 ESV

[21] The eye cannot say to the hand, "I have no need of you," nor again the head to the feet, "I have no need of you." [22] On the contrary, the parts of the body that seem to be weaker are indispensable, [23] and on those parts of the body that we think less honorable we bestow the greater honor, and our unpresentable parts are treated with greater modesty, [24] which our more presentable parts do not require. But God has so composed the body, giving greater honor to the part that lacked it, [25] that there may be no division in the body, but that the members may have the same care for one another. [26] If one member suffers, all suffer together; if one member is honored, all rejoice together.

1 Peter 4:10 ESV

[10] As each has received a gift, use it to serve one another, as good stewards of God's varied grace:

Prayer

Father, I ask You to reveal to me what my spiritual gifts are by Your Holy Spirit. Open my eyes so that I may see the vision that You have designed for my life. I realize that we were all created for a purpose; Lord, show me my purpose and calling I pray. Lord, lead, guide, and direct my path so that I may bring You the glory and honor due Your Holy name.

In Jesus name, I pray and ask it all,

Amen

Chosen by God

John 15:16 ESV

[16] You did not choose me, but I chose you and appointed you that you should go and bear fruit and that your fruit should abide, so that whatever you ask the Father in my name, he may give it to you.

Deuteronomy 7:6 ESV

"For you are a people holy to the LORD your God. The LORD your God has chosen you to be a people for his treasured possession, out of all the peoples who are on the face of the earth."

1 Peter 2:9 ESV

"But you are a chosen race, a royal priesthood, a holy nation, a people for his own possession, that you may proclaim the excellencies of him who called you out of darkness into his marvelous light."

Ephesians 1:3-10 ESV

3. Blessed be the God and Father of our Lord Jesus Christ, who has blessed us in Christ with every spiritual blessing in the heavenly places, 4. even as he chose us in him before the foundation of the world, that we should be holy and blameless before him. In love 5. he predestined us for adoption to himself as sons through Jesus Christ, according to the purpose of his will, 6. to the praise of his glorious grace, with which he has blessed us in the Beloved. 7. In him we have redemption through his blood, the forgiveness of our trespasses, according to the riches of his grace, 8. which he lavished upon us, in all wisdom and insight 9. making known to us the mystery of his will, according to his purpose, which he set forth in Christ 10. as a plan for the fullness of time, to unite all things in him, things in heaven and things on earth.

Psalm 139:17-18 AMP

How precious also are Your thoughts to me, O God! How vast is the sum of them! If I could count them, they would outnumber the sand. When I awake, I am still with You.

Psalm 139:17-18 AMP

How precious also are Your thoughts to me, O God! How vast is the sum of them! If I could count them, they would outnumber the sand. When I awake, I am still with You.

Psalm 8:3-4 ESV

[3] When I look at your heavens, the work of your fingers, the moon and the stars, which you have set in place, [4] what is man that you are mindful of him, and the son of man that you care for him?

1 Corinthians 1:9 AMP

"God is faithful [He is reliable, trustworthy and ever true to His promise-He can be depended on], and through Him you were called into fellowship with His Son, Jesus Christ our Lord."

Psalm 84:11 ESV

[11] For the LORD God is a sun and shield; the LORD bestows favor and honor. No good thing does he withhold from those who walk uprightly.

Thank You Father!

Prayer and Faith

As believers, we are called to have faith in God and His Son Jesus Christ, the Living Word. Faith is not just a mental agreement, but a heartfelt conviction that shapes our lives.

The Bible tells us in Hebrews 11:6 AMP:
[6] But without faith it is impossible to [walk with God and] please Him, for whoever comes [near] to God must [necessarily] believe that God exists and that He rewards those who [earnestly and diligently] seek Him.

Walking with God and pleasing Him are not optional but essential for our spiritual growth and well-being. But how do we walk with God and please Him? How do we develop a personal, intimate relationship with the true and living God?

In order to develop a personal, intimate relationship with the true and living God, three things are essential: The Holy Spirit, Prayer, and the Word of God.

The Holy Spirit:
God has given us the Holy Spirit to reveal His nature and His ways to us.

The Holy Spirit often communicates with us by putting a thought or an idea in our minds. Or He will guide us by stirring our hearts to speak, act, or think in alignment with God's will. He is also our teacher; Our Lord Jesus in his last conversation with his disciples before his crucifixion said, "But the Helper, the Holy Spirit, whom the Father will send in my name, he will teach you all things and bring to your remembrance all that I have said to you." (John 14:26 ESV)

John 3:3 ESV
Jesus answered him, "Truly, truly, I say to you, unless one is born again he cannot see the kingdom of God."

John 3: 5-6 ESV

[5] Jesus answered, "Truly, truly, I say to you, unless one is born of water and the spirit, he cannot enter the kingdom of God. [6] That which is born of the flesh is flesh, and that which is born of the Spirit is spirit.

Prayer:
The Key to Communication and Trust is Prayer

Prayer is how we communicate with God, express our needs and desires, and listen to His voice. It is also how we build trust in God, depend on Him, and receive His blessings. Prayer is not a ritual or a duty but a privilege and a joy.

God loves us with an everlasting love, a love that is unconditional and unchanging. He loves us not because of what we do or don't do but because of who He is. He is love, and He wants us to experience His love in a personal way. He invites us to come to Him as we are, with honesty and humility, and He promises to hear and answer us.

The Word of God is Key to Knowledge and Transformation

The Word of God is the revelation of God's character, will, and plan. It is not just a book but a living and powerful force that can change our lives. The Word of God is not just to be read but to be meditated on, applied, and obeyed.

The Word of God is the source of truth, wisdom, and guidance for every situation we face in this world. The Word of God is also the seed of God's promises, the promises that He has given us for our present and future. The Word of God is the food for our faith, the faith that pleases God and moves mountains.

But the Word of God does not work automatically in our lives. We need to plant it in our hearts, water it with prayer, and wait for it to bear fruit. We need to trust God's timing and His way, knowing that He is faithful and able to do exceedingly abundantly above all that we ask or think, according to His power that is at work within us (Ephesians 3:20-21 AMP) To Him be the glory in the church and in Christ Jesus throughout all generations forever and ever. Amen.

Let us therefore keep sowing the Word of God in our hearts, and let us walk by faith and not by sight, trusting in His timing and His will, that He might be glorified in our lives.

1 Thessalonians 5:16-18 ESV

Rejoice always, pray without ceasing, give thanks in all circumstances; for this is the will of God in Christ Jesus for you.

Psalm 100:4-5 ESV

Enter his gates with thanksgiving, and his courts with praise! Give thanks to him; bless his name! For the LORD is good; his steadfast love endures forever, and his faithfulness to all generations.

John 16:23-24 AMP

"In that day you will not [need to] ask Me about anything. I assure you and most solemnly say to you, whatever you ask the Father in My name [as My representative], He will give you. Until now you have not asked [the Father] for anything in My name; but now ask and keep on asking and you will receive, so that your joy may be full and complete."

James 5:16 ESV

"Therefore, confess your sins to one another and pray for one another, that you may be healed. The prayer of a righteous person has great power as it is working."

Thessalonians 3:16 ESV

[16] Now may the Lord of peace himself give you peace at all times in every way. The Lord be with you all.

1 Peter 5:6-7 ESV

[6] Humble yourselves, therefore, under the mighty hand of God so that at the proper time he may exalt you, [7] casting all your anxieties on him, because he cares for you.

John 15:7 ESV

"If you abide in me, and my words abide in you, ask whatever you wish, and it will be done for you."

Psalm 84:11 AMP

[11] For the LORD God is a sun and shield; The LORD bestows grace and favor and honor; No good thing will He withhold from those who walk uprightly.

1 John 5:14-15 ESV

"And this is the confidence that we have toward him, that if we ask anything according to his will he hears us. And if we know that he hears us in whatever we ask, we know that we have the requests that we have asked of him."

Hebrews 4:16 AMP

"Therefore let us [with privilege] approach the throne of grace [that is, the throne of God's gracious favor] with confidence and without fear, so that we may receive mercy [for our failures] and find [His amazing] grace to help in time of need [an appropriate blessing, coming just at the right moment]."

Matthew 18:19-20 ESV

"Again I say to you, if two of you agree on earth about anything they ask, it will be done for them by my Father in heaven. For where two or three are gathered in my name, there am I among them."

Proverbs 16:7 ESV

When a man's ways please the LORD, he makes even his enemies to be at peace with him.

Romans 8:26-28 ESV

[26] Likewise the Spirit helps us in our weakness. For we do not know what to pray for as we ought, but the Spirit himself intercedes for us with groanings too deep for words. [27] And he who searches hearts knows what is the mind of the Spirit, because the Spirit intercedes for the saints according to the will of God. [28] And we know that for those who love God all things work together for good, for those who are called according to his purpose.

Romans 12:12 ESV

Rejoice in hope, be patient in tribulation, be constant in prayer.

Philippians 4:6-7 ESV

Do not be anxious about anything, but in everything by prayer and supplication with thanksgiving let your requests be made known to God. And the peace of God, which surpasses all understanding, will guard your hearts and your minds in Christ Jesus.

Colossians 4:2 ESV

Continue steadfastly in prayer, being watchful in it with thanksgiving.

James 5:13 ESV

Is anyone among you suffering? Let him pray. Is anyone cheerful? Let him sing praise.

Matthew 6:33-34 ESV

But seek first the kingdom of God and his righteousness, and all these things will be added to you. "Therefore do not be anxious about tomorrow, for tomorrow will be anxious for itself. Sufficient for the day is its own trouble.

3 John 1:2 AMP

Beloved, I pray that in every way you may succeed and prosper and be in good health [physically], just as [I know] your soul prospers [spiritually].

Psalm 69:13 AMP

But as for me, my prayer is to You, O LORD, at an acceptable and opportune time; O God, in the greatness of Your favor and in the abundance of Your lovingkindness, Answer me with truth [that is, the faithfulness of Your salvation].

Psalm 66:19-20 ESV

But truly God has listened; he has attended to the voice of my prayer. Blessed be God, because he has not rejected my prayer or removed his steadfast love from me!

Matthew 6:14-15 AMP

For if you forgive others their trespasses [their reckless and willful sins], your heavenly Father will also forgive you. But if you do not forgive others [nurturing your hurt and anger with the result that it interferes with your relationship with God], then your Father will not forgive your trespasses.

John 14:13-14 ESV

"Whatever you ask in my name, this I will do, that the Father may be glorified in the Son. If you ask me anything in my name, I will do it."

Psalm 37:4 ESV

"Delight yourself in the LORD, and he will give you the desires of your heart."

Matthew 6:6 ESV

"But when you pray, go into your room and shut the door and pray to your Father who is in secret. And your Father who sees in secret will reward you."

Psalm 50:15 AMP

"Call on Me in the day of trouble; I will rescue you, and you shall honor and glorify Me."

2 Chronicles 7:14 ESV

"If my people who are called by my name humble themselves, and pray and seek my face and turn from their wicked ways, then I will hear from heaven and will forgive their sin and heal their land."

Mark 11:24-26 ESV

"Therefore I tell you, whatever you ask in prayer, believe that you have received it, and it will be yours. And whenever you stand praying, forgive, if you have anything against anyone, so that your Father also who is in heaven may forgive you your trespasses."

Mark 9:23 AMP

Jesus said to him, "[You say to Me,] 'If You can?' All things are possible for the one who believes and trusts [in Me]!"

Isaiah 65:24 ESV

"Before they call I will answer; while they are yet speaking I will hear."

Matthew 21:22 ESV

"And whatever you ask in prayer, you will receive, if you have faith."

Jeremiah 29:12-13 ESV

"Then you will call upon me and come and pray to me, and I will hear you. You will seek me and find me, when you seek me with all your heart."

Matthew 7:7-8 ESV

"Ask, and it will be given to you; seek, and you will find; knock, and it will be opened to you. For everyone who asks receives, and the one who seeks finds, and to the one who knocks it will be opened.

Proverbs 15:29 ESV

The LORD is far from the wicked, but he hears the prayer of the righteous.

Psalm 102:17 AMP

He has regarded the prayer of the destitute, And has not despised their prayer.

Isaiah 41:10 AMP

"**Do not fear [anything], for I am with you; Do not be afraid, for I am your God. I will strengthen you, be assured I will help you; I will certainly take hold of you with My righteous right hand [a hand of justice, of power, of victory, of salvation].**"

Do not Fear Anything.

What if I receive a bad report from the doctor? What if it's serious, even worse, what if it's concerning a loved one? What if I was just laid off from my job, my son had just been arrested, or my ministry membership dropped fifty percent? God's word tells us not to fear ANYTHING; Do not be afraid.

If I were to list all the reasons why we do not need to fear, this book would not have enough pages to contain them all.

He is the King of Glory, all-powerful, all-knowing, able to do the impossible, the creator of the heavens and the earth and the fullness thereof. He is our healer (Jehovah Rapha), our provider (Jehovah Jireh), our peace (Jehovah Shalom), and our banner of victory (Jehovah Nissi).

He is our God, and He has promised never to leave you or forsake you. Whatever trials we go through, God is saying in Isaiah 41:10, I am your God. I will strengthen you; be assured I will help you; I will certainly take hold of you with My righteous right hand [a hand of justice, of power, of victory, and salvation].

He is "I AM"; In Him, we live and breathe and have our being. He has given all power in heaven and on earth to Jesus (Matthew 28:18-20); because of the finished work of Jesus Christ, we can now come boldly to the throne of Grace and obtain mercy and find grace to help in our time of need, (Hebrews 4:16).

Psalm 23:1, 4 ESV

[1] The Lord is my shepherd; I shall not want.

[4] Even though I walk through the valley in the shadow of death, I will fear no evil, for You are with me; Your rod and your staff they comfort me.

2 Timothy 1:7 AMP

[7] For God did not give us a spirit not of timidity or cowardice or fear, but of power and of love and of sound judgment and personal discipline [abilities that result in a calm, well-balanced mind and self-control.

Jeremiah 29:12-14 ESV

The Bible says, "Then you will call upon me and come and pray to me, and I will hear you. You will seek me and find me, when you seek me with all your heart. I will be found by you, declares the LORD ..."

Faith Comes From Hearing

Prayers in the Bible

Prayer is not just a method but a relationship. It is how we talk to our Father God, who created us, adopted us, and loves us eternally. Prayer is how we express our total reliance on Him, but also how we align our desires with His plan. But how can we discern His will and plan for our lives? The key is simple: if we are born again, then we have the Holy Spirit living in our hearts, and we have the mind of Christ. His Word, which is "a lamp unto our feet and a light unto our path," will guide us in prayer.

Jesus said to God the Father, before going to the cross, "Not my will but Your will be done." Luke 22:42. Included in God's will is His perfect timing. Numerous times during Jesus' ministry, He made statements like, "My hour has not yet come," John 2:4, or "I must work the works of Him that sent me..." John 9:4. Why? Because He understood that

He was working on a divine schedule, doing the will of the Father, and conforming to His timetable. Like Jesus, we would do well to consider that in our prayer life.

What is God's will concerning this matter? What has He said in His word concerning this situation? When we pray, we are saying, "Lord, I am turning this situation over to You."

If it is God's will, then we need to trust His timing (this is the hard part) because it's how we wait that's important. Are we pacing and checking the time? Or do we trust and believe that God is faithful and rest in that?

Jesus Prayed for Us

John 17:9-11 ESV

[9] I am praying for them. I am not praying for the world but for those whom you have given me, for they are yours. [10] All mine are yours, and yours are mine, and I am glorified in them. [11] And I am no longer in the world, but they are in the world, and I am coming to you. Holy Father,

keep them in your name, which you have given me, that they may be one, even as we are one.

Hebrews 7:25

[25] Consequently, he is able to save to the uttermost those who draw near to God through Him, since He always lives to make intercession for them.

A Prayer of Blessings

Numbers 6:22-27 ESV

[22] The LORD spoke to Moses, saying, [23] "Speak to Aaron and his sons, saying, Thus you shall bless the people of Israel: you shall say to them, [24] The LORD bless you and keep you; [25] the LORD make his face to shine upon you and be gracious to you; [26] the LORD lift up his countenance upon you and give you peace. [27] "So shall they put my name upon the people of Israel, and I will bless them."

Psalm 20:4-5 ESV

[4] May he grant you your heart's desire and fulfill all your plans! [5] May we shout for joy over your salvation, and in the name of our God set up our banners! May the LORD fulfill all your petitions!

The Lord's Prayer

Matthew 6:9-13 AMP

[9] "Pray, then, in this way: 'Our Father who is in heaven, Hallowed be Your name. [10] 'Your kingdom come, Your will be done On earth as it is in heaven. [11] 'Give us this day our daily bread. [12] 'And forgive us our debts, as we have forgiven our debtors [letting go of both the wrong and the resentment]. [13] 'And do not lead us into temptation, but deliver us from evil. [For Yours is the kingdom and the power and the glory forever. Amen.]'

Hallowed means set apart, kept and treated as holy, revere. Your Kingdom come, a plea for God's kingdom to be inaugurated on earth. Your will be done, including what God wishes to be done by the individual believer—His commands and precepts.

Our Daily Bread, life's essentials.

Forgive us our debts, sins, moral failures.

Do not lead us into temptation, lead us away from situations where we are vulnerable and have the opportunity to sin. God does not tempt man (see James 1:13) but does allow man to be tested.

But deliver us from evil, Or the evil one.

Jesus Prays in Gethsemane

Matthew 26:38-44 ESV

[38] Then he said to them, "My soul is very sorrowful, even to death; remain here, and watch with me." [39] And going a little farther he fell on his face and prayed, saying, "My Father, if it be possible, let this cup pass from me; nevertheless, not as I will, but as you will." [40] And he came to the disciples and found them sleeping. And he said to Peter, "So, could you not watch with me one hour? [41] Watch and pray that you may not enter into temptation.

The spirit indeed is willing, but the flesh is weak." [42] Again, for the second time, he went away and prayed, "My Father, if this cannot pass unless I drink it, your will be done." [43] And again he came and found them sleeping, for their eyes were heavy. [44] So, leaving them again, he went away and prayed for the third time, saying the same words again.

King Hezekiah's Prayer

2 Kings 19:14-19 ESV

[14] Hezekiah received the letter from the hand of the messengers and read it; and Hezekiah went up to the house of the LORD and spread it before the LORD. [15] And Hezekiah prayed before the LORD and said: "O LORD, the God of Israel, enthroned above the cherubim, you are the God, you alone, of all the kingdoms of the earth; you have made heaven and earth. [16] Incline your ear, O LORD, and hear; open your eyes, O LORD, and see; and hear the words of Sennacherib, which he has sent to mock the living God. [17] Truly, O LORD, the kings of Assyria have laid waste the nations and their lands [18] and have cast their gods into the fire, for they were not gods, but the work of men's hands, wood and stone. Therefore they were

destroyed. [19] So now, O LORD our God, save us, please, from his hand, that all the kingdoms of the earth may know that you, O LORD, are God alone."

Jabez Prayer

1 Chronicles 4:9-10 ESV

[9] Jabez was more honorable than his brothers; and his mother called his name Jabez, saying, "Because I bore him in pain." [10] Jabez called upon the God of Israel, saying, "Oh that you would bless me and enlarge my border, and that your hand might be with me, and that you would keep me from harm so that it might not bring me pain!" And God granted what he asked.

Jehoshaphat's Prayer

2 Chronicles 20:3-12 ESV

[3] Then Jehoshaphat was afraid and set his face to seek the LORD, and proclaimed a fast throughout all Judah. [4] And Judah assembled to seek help from the LORD; from all the cities of Judah they came to seek the LORD. [5] And Jehoshaphat stood in the assembly of Judah and Jerusalem, in the house of the LORD, before the new court, [6] and said, "O LORD, God of our fathers, are you not God in heaven? You rule over all the kingdoms of the nations. In your hand are power and might, so that none is able to withstand you. [7] Did you not, our God, drive out the inhabitants of this land before your people Israel, and give it forever to the descendants of Abraham your friend? [8] And they have lived in it and have built for you in it a sanctuary for your name, saying, [9] 'If disaster comes upon us, the sword, judgment, or pestilence, or famine, we will stand before this house and before you-for your name is in this house-and cry out to you in our affliction, and you will hear and save.' [10] And now behold, the men of Ammon and Moab and Mount Seir, whom you would not let Israel invade when they came from the land of Egypt, and whom they avoided and did not destroy- [11] behold,

they reward us by coming to drive us out of your possession, which you have given us to inherit. [12] O our God, will you not execute judgment on them? For we are powerless against this great horde that is coming against us. We do not know what to do, but our eyes are on you."

There are lessons to be learned from each one of these prayers; my prayer for you is that as you grow closer to God in your daily walk, you will adopt and model these prayers.

Faith Comes From Hearing

Salvation

Good News!

Romans Road is a way of understanding salvation, based on the fact that we all need salvation, because we have all sinned and are accountable to God. We all fall short of God's holiness and righteousness, and that is why we need a savior. Sin separated us from God. Jesus Christ is the atoning sacrifice for our sins, and if you have accepted the gift of salvation, through Him you can be saved and be in a right relationship with God who is Holy. This is the Good News.

Why We Need Salvation

1. Romans 3:23 ESV

[23] for all have sinned and fall short of the glory of God,

2. Romans 5:8 AMP

[8] But God clearly shows and proves His own love for us, by the fact that while we were still sinners, Christ died for us.

3. Romans 6:23 ESV

[23] For the wages of sin is death, but the free gift of God is eternal life in Christ Jesus our Lord.

4. Romans 8:1 AMP

[1] Therefore there is now no condemnation [no guilty verdict, no punishment] for those who are in Christ Jesus [who believe in Him as personal Lord and Savior].

Romans 10:9 AMP

[9] because if you acknowledge and confess with your mouth that Jesus is Lord [recognizing His power, authority, and majesty as God], and believe in your heart that God raised Him from the dead, you will be saved.

Romans 5:1-2 AMP

[1] Therefore, since we have been justified [that is, acquitted of sin, declared blameless before God] by faith, [let us grasp the fact that] we have peace with God [and the joy of reconciliation with Him] through our Lord Jesus Christ (the Messiah, the Anointed). [2] Through Him we also have access by faith into this [remarkable state of] grace in which we [firmly and safely and securely] stand. Let us rejoice in our hope and the confident assurance of [experiencing and enjoying] the glory of [our great] God [the manifestation of His excellence and power].

Hebrews 1:3 ESV

[3] He is the radiance of the glory of God and the exact imprint of his nature, and he upholds the universe by the word of his power. After making purification for sins, he sat down at the right hand of the Majesty on high,

Hebrews 1:3-4 AMP

[3] The Son is the radiance and only expression of the glory of [our awesome] God [reflecting God's Shekinah glory, the Light-being, the brilliant light of the divine], and the exact representation and perfect imprint of His [Father's] essence, and upholding and maintaining and propelling all things [the entire physical and spiritual universe] by His powerful word [carrying the universe along to its predetermined goal]. When He [Himself and no other] had [by offering Himself on the cross as a sacrifice for sin] accomplished purification from sins and established our freedom from guilt, He sat down [revealing His completed work] at the right hand of the Majesty on high [revealing His Divine Authority], [4] having become as much superior as angels, since He has inherited a more excellent and glorious name than they [that is, Son-the name above all names].

John 1:14 ESV

[14] And the Word became flesh and dwelt among us, and we have seen his glory, glory as of the only Son from the Father, full of grace and truth.

John 1:14 AMP

[14] And the Word (Christ) became flesh, and lived among us; and we [actually] saw His glory, glory as belongs to the [One and] only begotten Son of the Father, [the Son who is truly unique, the only One of His kind, who is] full of grace and truth (absolutely free of deception).

Faith Comes From Hearing

God is With Us

Psalm 139:7-12 AMP

[7] Where can I go from Your Spirit? Or where can I flee from Your presence? [8] If I ascend to heaven, You are there; If I make my bed in Sheol (the nether world, the place of the dead), behold, You are there. [9] If I take the wings of the dawn, If I dwell in the remotest part of the sea, [10] Even there Your hand will lead me, And Your right hand will take hold of me. [11] If I say, "Surely the darkness will cover me, And the night will be the only light around me," [12] Even the darkness is not dark to You and conceals nothing from You, But the night shines as bright as the day; Darkness and light are alike to You.

Jonah 2:1-2 ESV

[1] Then Jonah prayed to the LORD his God from the belly of the fish, [2] saying, "I called out to the LORD, out of my distress, and he answered me; out of the belly of Sheol I cried, and you heard my voice.

Psalm 139:13-16 AMP

[13] For You formed my innermost parts; You knit me [together] in my mother's womb. [14] I will give thanks and praise to You, for I am fearfully and wonderfully made; Wonderful are Your works, And my soul knows it very well. [15] My frame was not hidden from You, When I was being formed in secret, And intricately and skillfully formed [as if embroidered with many colors] in the depths of the earth. [16] Your eyes have seen my unformed substance; And in Your book were all written The days that were appointed for me, When as yet there was not one of them [even taking shape].

Issues of Life

Anger

James 1:19-22 AMP

[19] Understand this, my beloved brothers and sisters. Let everyone be quick to hear [be a careful, thoughtful listener], slow to speak [a speaker of carefully chosen words and], slow to anger [patient, reflective, forgiving]; [20] for the resentful, deep-seated] anger of man does not produce the righteousness of God [that standard of behavior which He requires from us]. [21] So get rid of all uncleanness and all that remains of wickedness, and with a humble spirit receive the word [of God] which is implanted [actually rooted in your heart], which is able to save your souls. [22] But prove yourselves doers of the word [actively and continually obeying God's precepts], and not merely listeners [who hear the word but fail to internalize its meaning], deluding yourselves [by unsound reasoning contrary to the truth].

Psalm 145:8 AMP

[8] The LORD is gracious and full of compassion, Slow to anger and abounding in lovingkindness.

James 1:19-21 ESV

[19] Know this, my beloved brothers: let every person be quick to hear, slow to speak, slow to anger; [20] for the anger of man does not produce the righteousness of God. [21] Therefore put away all filthiness and rampant wickedness and receive with meekness the implanted word, which is able to save your souls. [22] But be doers of the word, and not hearers only, deceiving yourselves.

Proverbs 15:1 ESV

[1] A soft answer turns away wrath, but a harsh word stirs up anger.

Colossians 3:21 AMP

[21] Fathers, do not provoke or irritate or exasperate your children [with demands that are trivial or unreasonable or humiliating or abusive; nor by favoritism or indifference; treat them tenderly with lovingkindness], so they will not lose heart and become discouraged or unmotivated [with their spirits broken].

Ephesians 4:26-27 AMP

[26] BE ANGRY [at sin-at immorality, at injustice, at ungodly behavior], YET DO NOT SIN; do not let your anger [cause you shame, nor allow it to] last until the sun goes down. [27] And do not give the devil an opportunity [to lead you into sin by holding a grudge, or nurturing anger, or harboring resentment, or cultivating bitterness].

Romans 12:19-21 ESV

[19] Beloved, never avenge yourselves, but leave it to the wrath of God, for it is written, "Vengeance is mine, I will repay, says the Lord." [20] To the contrary, "if your enemy is hungry, feed him; if he is thirsty, give him something to drink; for by so doing you will heap burning coals on his head." [21] Do not be overcome by evil, but overcome evil with good.

Proverbs 13:10 AMP

[10] Through pride and presumption come nothing but strife, But [skillful and godly] wisdom is with those who welcome [well-advised] counsel.

Faith

In the Bible, the words "faith" and "belief" are closely related but not identical. "Belief" is an acceptance that a statement is true or that something exists; one may believe in the historical existence of Jesus Christ.

On the other hand, "faith" is often associated with trust and action. It is not just believing in God's existence but also trusting in God's promises and living out that trust. The biblical definition of faith, as found in Hebrews 11:1, is "confidence in what we hope for and assurance about what we do not see." This implies a deeper level of commitment than mere belief.

In practical terms, belief can be seen as the first step, which may then lead to faith, which is belief in action. Faith, according to James 2:17, is demonstrated by actions: "In the same way, faith by itself, if it is not accompanied by action, is dead." This suggests that faith goes beyond belief to include the trust and action that flow from belief.

So, while belief and faith are related concepts in the Bible, faith encompasses a fuller experience that includes belief, trust, and action.

Hebrews 11:1-3, 6 ESV

Now faith is the assurance of things hoped for, the conviction of things not seen. [2] For by it the people of old received their commendation. [3] By faith we understand that the universe was created by the word of God, so that what is seen was not made out of things that are visible. [6] And without faith it is impossible to please Him [God], for whoever would draw near to God must believe that He exists and that He rewards those who seek Him.

Matthews17:20 ESV

He said to them, "Because of your little faith. For truly, I say to you, if you have faith like a grain of mustard seed, you will say to this mountain, 'Move from here to there,' and it will move, and nothing will be impossible for you.

Moving a mountain was a common metaphor in Jewish literature for doing what seemed impossible.

Romans 1:16-17 ESV

For I am not ashamed of the gospel, for it is the power of God for salvation to everyone who believes, to the Jew first and also to the Greek. [17] For in it the righteousness of God is revealed from faith to faith, as it is written, "The righteous shall live by faith."

Ephesians 2:8-10 ESV

For by grace you have been saved through faith. And this is not your own doing; it is the gift of God, [9] not a result of works, so that no man may boast. [10] For we are His workmanship, created in Christ Jesus for good works, which God prepared beforehand, that we should walk in them.

6:35 ESV

[35] Jesus said to them, "I am the bread of life; whoever comes to me shall not hunger, and whoever believes in me shall never thirst.

Mark 9:23-24 AMP

[23] Jesus said to him, "[You say to Me,] 'If You can?' All things are possible for the one who believes and trusts [in Me]!" [24] Immediately the father of the boy cried out [with a desperate, piercing cry], saying, "I do believe; help [me overcome] my unbelief."

Acts 16:30-31 ESV

[30] Then he brought them out and said, "Sirs, what must I do to be saved?" [31] And they said, "Believe in the Lord Jesus, and you will be saved, you and your household."

John 1:12-13 ESV

[12] But to all who did receive him, who believed in his name, he gave the right to become children of God, [13] who were born, not of blood nor of the will of the flesh nor of the will of man, but of God.

John 3:36 ESV

[36] Whoever believes in the Son has eternal life; whoever does not obey the Son shall not see life, but the wrath of God remains on him.

John 3:16 ESV

[16] "For God so loved the world, that he gave his only Son, that whoever believes in him should not perish but have eternal life.

1 Peter 1:6-7 ESV

In this you rejoice, though now for a little while, if necessary, you have been grieved by various trials, [7] so that the tested genuiness of your faith-more precious than gold that perishes though it is tested by fire-may be found to result in praise and glory and honor at the revelation of Jesus Christ.

Comfort and Peace

Psalm 46:1-3,7 ESV

God is our refuge and strength, a very present help in trouble. [2] Therefore we will not fear though the earth gives way, though the mountains be moved into the heart of the sea, [3] though its waters roar and foam, though the mountains tremble at its swelling. Selah [7] The LORD of

hosts is with us; the God of Jacob is our fortress. Selah

Psalm 18:2-3 AMP

[2] The LORD is my rock, my fortress, and the One who rescues me; My God, my rock and strength in whom I trust and take refuge; My shield, and the horn of my salvation, my high tower-my stronghold. [3] I call upon the LORD, who is worthy to be praised; And I am saved from my enemies.

Psalm 22:24 AMP

[24] For He has not despised nor detested the suffering of the afflicted; Nor has He hidden His face from him; But when he cried to Him for help, He listened.

Nahum 1:7 ESV

[7] The LORD is good, a stronghold in the day of trouble; he knows those who take refuge in him.

Psalm 55:22 AMP

[22] Cast your burden on the LORD [release it] and He will sustain and uphold you; He will never allow the righteous to be shaken (slip, fall, fail).

John 16:33 AMP

[33] I have told you these things, so that in Me you may have [perfect] peace. In the world you have tribulation and distress and suffering, but be courageous [be confident, be undaunted, be filled with joy]; I have overcome the world."

[My conquest is accomplished, My victory abiding.]

Psalm 27:13-14 AMP

[13] I would have despaired had I not believed that I would see the goodness of the LORD In the land of the living. [14] Wait for and confidently expect the LORD; Be strong and let your heart take courage; Yes, wait for and confidently expect the LORD.

Proverbs 27:17 AMP

[17] As iron sharpens iron, So one man sharpens [and influences] another [through discussion].

Christian Living

Matthew 22:36-40 ESV

[36] "Teacher, which is the great commandment in the Law?" [37] And he said to him, "You shall love the Lord your God with all your heart and with all your soul and with all your mind. [38] This is the great and first commandment. [39] And a second is like it: You shall love your neighbor as yourself. [40] On these two commandments depend all the Law and the Prophets."

Matthew 5:14-16 ESV

[14] "You are the light of the world. A city set on a hill cannot be hidden. [15] Nor do people light a lamp and put it under a basket, but on a stand, and it gives light to all in the house. [16] In the same way, let your light shine before others, so that they may see your good works and give glory to your Father who is in heaven.

Matthew 6:33 AMP

[33] But first and most importantly seek (aim at, strive after) His kingdom and His righteousness [His way of doing and being right-the attitude and character of God], and all these things will be given to you also.

Matthew 6:14-15 ESV

[14] For if you forgive others their trespasses, your heavenly Father will also forgive you, [15] but if you do not forgive others their trespasses, neither will your Father forgive your trespasses.

1 Thessalonians 5:16-18 ESV

[16] Rejoice always, [17] pray without ceasing, [18] give thanks in all circumstances; for this is the will of God in Christ Jesus for you.

James 1:19-20 ESV

[19] Know this, my beloved brothers: let every person be quick to hear, slow to speak, slow to anger; [20] for the anger of man does not produce the righteousness of God.

Matthew 5:23-24 AMP

[23] So if you are presenting your offering at the altar, and while there you remember that your brother has something [such as a grievance or legitimate complaint] against you, [24] leave your offering there at the altar and go. First make peace with your brother, and then come and present your offering.

Matthew 25:35-40 ESV

[35] For I was hungry and you gave me food, I was thirsty and you gave me drink, I was a stranger and you welcomed me, [36] I was naked and you clothed me, I was sick and you visited me, I was in prison and you came to me.' [37] Then the righteous will answer him, saying, 'Lord, when did we see you hungry and feed you, or thirsty and give you drink? [38] And when did we see you a stranger and welcome you, or naked and clothe you? [39] And when did we see you sick or in prison and visit you?' [40] And the King will answer them, 'Truly, I say to you, as you did it to one of the least of these my brothers, you did it to me.'

Colossians 3:23-24 AMP

[23] Whatever you do [whatever your task may be], work from the soul [that is, put in your very best effort], as [something done] for the Lord and not for men,

Colossians 3:24 AMP

[24] knowing [with all certainty] that it is from the Lord [not from men] that you will receive the inheritance which is your [greatest] reward. It is the Lord Christ whom you [actually] serve.

2 Corinthians 9:6-7 ESV

[6] The point is this: whoever sows sparingly will also reap sparingly, and whoever sows bountifully will also reap bountifully. [7] Each one must give as he has decided in his heart, not reluctantly or under compulsion, for God loves a cheerful giver

Philippians 2:14-15 ESV

[14] Do all things without grumbling or disputing, [15] that you may be blameless and innocent, children of God without blemish in the midst of a crooked and twisted generation, among whom you shine as lights in the world...

Colossians 3:18-21 AMP

[18] Wives, be subject to your husbands [out of respect for their position as protector, and their accountability to God], as is proper and fitting in the Lord. [19] Husbands, love your wives [with an affectionate, sympathetic, selfless love that always seeks the best for them] and do not be embittered or resentful toward them [because of the responsibilities of marriage]. [20] Children, obey your parents [as God's representatives] in all things, for this [attitude of respect and obedience] is well-pleasing to the Lord [and will bring you God's promised blessings]. [21] Fathers, do not provoke or irritate or exasperate your children [with demands that are trivial or unreasonable or humiliating or abusive; nor by favoritism or indifference; treat them tenderly with lovingkindness], so they will not lose heart and become discouraged or unmotivated [with their spirits broken].

Luke 6:37-38 ESV

[37] "Judge not, and you will not be judged; condemn not, and you will not be condemned; forgive, and you will be forgiven; [38] give, and it will be given to you. Good measure, pressed down, shaken together, running over, will be put into your lap. For with the measure you use it will be measured back to you."

Matthew 28:16-20 ESV

[16] Now the eleven disciples went to Galilee, to the mountain to which Jesus had directed them. [17] And when they saw him they worshiped him, but some doubted. [18] And Jesus came and said to them, "All authority in heaven and on earth has been given to me. [19] Go therefore and make disciples of all nations, baptizing them in the name of the Father and of the Son and of the Holy Spirit, [20] teaching them to observe all that I have commanded you. And behold, I am with you always, to the end of the age."

Ephesians 5:1-4 ESV

[1] Therefore be imitators of God, as beloved children. [2] And walk in love, as Christ loved us and gave himself up for us, a fragrant offering and sacrifice to God. [3] But sexual immorality and all impurity or covetousness must not even be named among you, as is proper among saints. [4] Let there be no filthiness nor foolish talk nor crude joking, which are out of place, but instead let there be thanksgiving.

God's Correction

There are so many misconceptions, so much of the time; God is accused unjustly by unbelievers as well as believers: for taking a loved one too soon, for allowing children to suffer with sickness, for some to be destitute while others have millions or billions, and all the injustice that goes on in the world. All those who believe this way do not know God and have not read with understanding His word. I want to make two points and strongly recommend that you let God's word speak for itself as you enter a deeper, intimate relationship with the creator of the universe.

First, God is love; everything He does is motivated by love; look at John 3:16 for instance. [16] "For God so loved the world, that he gave his only Son, that whoever believes in him should not perish but have eternal life. Sin is the culprit, and since we have both free will and sinful nature, sin came into the world, but because God is omniscient, meaning all-knowing, He already had a plan. Sin separated us from God. We see that in the Garden of Eden, with the first man, Adam. Jesus is our atonement for sin. John 3:17 ESV [17] For God did not send his Son into the world to condemn the world, but in order that the world might be saved through him. The world is cursed because of sin, but not only that, we have an adversary in Satan. The Bible says this about him: John 10:10 ESV [10] The thief comes only to steal and kill and destroy. I came that they may have life and have it abundantly. Here, he's described as a thief. In other places throughout the New Testament, Satan is referred to as a "tempter" (Matthew 4:3), "the ruler of the demons" (Matthew 12:24), "the God of this Age" (2 Corinthians 4:4), "the evil one" (1 John 5:18), and "a roaring lion" (1 Peter 5:8). he called the father of lies, etc.,

My point is this: sin is the Enemy's authority and power to steal, kill, and destroy. Fortunately, we have an advocate who is sitting on the right hand of the throne of God, who forever lives to intercede for the believer (saints).

John 3:3 ESV

[3] Jesus answered him, "Truly, truly, I say to you, unless one is born again, he cannot see the kingdom of God."

I realize that these words do not fully explain God's plan of salvation, but it's my prayer that this book will direct you to the source of all wisdom and knowledge- His Holy Word, the Bible.

My second point: The Kingdom of heaven is both now and future, meaning that there are benefits to being a part of it now on earth, but the most glorious benefits will occur when we get to heaven. This world, our life, is temporal, and this is not our home. We came from heaven, where God created our souls, and when we take our last breath on this side, we will return to our maker.

Ecclesiastes 12:7 ESV

[7] and the dust returns to the earth as it was, and the spirit returns to God who gave it. John 15:19 ESV [19] If you were of the world, the world would love you as its own; but because you are not of the world, but I chose you out of the world, therefore the world hates you. Philippians 3:20-21 NLT [20] But we are citizens of heaven, where the Lord

Jesus Christ lives. And we are eagerly waiting for him to return as our Savior. [21] He will take our weak mortal bodies and change them into glorious bodies like his own, using the same power with which he will bring everything under his control.

This world is not our home; we are pilgrims on a journey. This verse teaches us that our life on earth is temporary and our real destination is heaven. Jesus himself instructed us to: John 14:1 ESV [1] Let not your hearts be troubled. Believe in God; believe also in me.

Why is God telling you to let not your heart be troubled? God is telling you, "Let not your heart be troubled" because He loves you and cares for you. He knows what you are going through, and He has a plan for your life. He wants you to trust Him and His promises and to have peace and joy in Him. He does not want you to be anxious or afraid but to cast all your worries on Him because He is able to help you and deliver you. He is with you always and He will never leave you nor forsake you. He is your refuge and strength, your hope, and your salvation.

John 16:33 ESV

[33] I have said these things to you, that in me you may have peace. In the world you will have tribulation. But take heart; I have overcome the world."

Proverbs 3:12 AMP

[12] For those whom the LORD loves He corrects, Even as a father corrects the son in whom he delights.

2 Timothy 3:16-17 ESV

[16] All Scripture is breathed out by God and profitable for teaching, for reproof, for correction, and for training in righteousness, [17] that the man of God may be complete, equipped for every good work.

Hebrews 12:7-10 AMP

[7] You must submit to [correction for the purpose of] discipline; God is dealing with you as with sons; for what son is there whom his father does not discipline? [8] Now if you are exempt from correction and without discipline, in which all [of God's children] share, then you are illegitimate children and not sons [at all].

Hebrews 5:7-10 ESV

[7] In the days of his flesh, Jesus offered up prayers and supplications, with loud cries and tears, to him who was able to save him from death, and he was heard because of his reverence. [8] Although he was a son, he learned obedience through what he suffered. [9] And being made perfect, he became the source of eternal salvation to all who obey him, [10] being designated by God a high priest after the order of Melchizedek.

1 Peter 5:9-10 AMP

[9] But resist him, be firm in your faith [against his attack rooted, established, immovable], knowing that the same experiences of suffering are being experienced by your brothers and sisters throughout the world. [You do not suffer alone.] [10] After you have suffered for a little while, the God of all grace [who imparts His blessing and favor], who called you to His own eternal glory in Christ, will Himself complete, confirm, strengthen, and establish you [making you what you ought to be].

Proverbs 18:12 AMP

[12] Before disaster the heart of a man is haughty and filled with self-importance, But humility comes before honor.

Psalm 121:1-2 ESV

[1] I lift up my eyes to the hills. From where does my help come? [2] My help comes from the LORD, who made heaven and earth.

Psalm 84:10 ESV

[10] For a day in your courts is better than a thousand elsewhere. I would rather be a doorkeeper in the house of my God than dwell in the tents of wickedness.

James 4:11-12 ESV

[10] Do not speak evil against one another, brothers. The one who speaks against a brother or judges his brother, speaks evil against the law and judges the law. But if you judge the law, you are not a doer of the law but a judge. [12] There is only one lawgiver and judge, he who is able to save and to destroy. But who are you to judge your neighbor?

Isaiah 26:3 AMP

[3] "You will keep in perfect and constant peace the one whose mind is steadfast [that is, committed and focused on You-in both inclination and character], Because he trusts and takes refuge in You [with hope and confident expectation].

James 4:7-8 ESV

[7] Submit yourselves therefore to God. Resist the devil, and he will flee from you. [8] Draw near to God, and he will draw near to you. Cleanse your hands, you sinners, and purify your hearts, you double-minded.

Proverbs 3:3-4 AMP

[3] Do not let mercy and kindness and truth leave you [instead let these qualities define you]; Bind them [securely] around your neck, Write them on the tablet of your heart. [4] So find favor and high esteem In the sight of God and man.

John 15:18-19 ESV

[18] "If the world hates you, know that it has hated me before it hated you. [19] If you were of the world, the world would love you as its own; but because you are not of the world, but I chose you out of the world, therefore the world hates you.

Philippians 4:4-5 AMP

[4] Rejoice in the Lord always [delight, take pleasure in Him]; again I will say, rejoice! [5] Let your gentle spirit [your graciousness, unselfishness, mercy, tolerance, and patience] be known to all people. The Lord is near.

Prayer for the Church

1 Corinthians 1:3-9 ESV

Grace to you and peace from God our Father and the Lord Jesus Christ. I give thanks to my God always for you because of the grace of God that was given you in Christ Jesus, that in every way you were enriched in him in all speech and all knowledge- even as the testimony about Christ was confirmed among you- so that you are not lacking in any gift, as you wait for the revealing of our Lord Jesus Christ, who will sustain you to the end, guiltless in the day of our Lord Jesus Christ. God is faithful, by whom you were called into the fellowship of his Son, Jesus Christ our Lord.

Philippians 1:8-11 ESV

[8] For God is my witness, how I yearn for you all with the affection of Christ Jesus. [9] And it is my prayer that your love may abound more and more, with knowledge and all discernment, [10] so that you may approve what is excellent, and so be pure and blameless for the day of Christ, [11] filled with the fruit of righteousness that comes through Jesus Christ, to the glory and praise of God.

Ephesians 3:14-19 ESV

[14] For this reason I bow my knees before the Father, [15] from whom every family in heaven and on earth is named, [16] that according to the riches of his glory he may grant you to be strengthened with power through his Spirit in your inner being, [17] so that Christ may dwell in your hearts through faith-that you, being rooted and grounded in love, [18] may have strength to comprehend with all the saints what is the breadth and length and height and depth, [19] and to know the love of Christ that surpasses knowledge, that you may be filled with all the fullness of God.

Ephesians 1:15-21 ESV

[15] For this reason, because I have heard of your faith in the Lord Jesus and your love toward all the saints, [16] I do not cease to give thanks for you, remembering you in my prayers, [17] that the God of our Lord Jesus Christ, the Father of glory, may give you the Spirit of wisdom and of revelation in the knowledge of him, [18] having the eyes of your hearts enlightened, that you may know what is the hope to which he has called you, what are the riches of his glorious inheritance in the saints, [19] and what is the immeasurable greatness of his power toward us who believe, according to the working of his great might [20] that he worked in Christ when he raised him from the dead and seated him at his right hand in the heavenly places, [21] far above all rule and authority and power and dominion, and above every name that is named, not only in this age but also in the one to come.

Faith Comes From Hearing

The Glory of God

Jude 1:24-25 ESV

[24] Now to him who is able to keep you from stumbling and to present you blameless before the presence of his glory with great joy, [25] to the only God, our Savior, through Jesus Christ our Lord, be glory, majesty, dominion, and authority, before all time and now and forever.
Amen.

Ephesians 3:20-21 ESV

[20] Now to him who is able to do far more abundantly than all that we ask or think, according to the power at work within us, [21] to him be glory in the church and in Christ Jesus throughout all generations, forever and ever. Amen.

Luke 2:14 AMP

[14] "Glory to God in the highest [heaven], And on earth peace among men with whom He is well-pleased."

1 Chronicles 29:11-13 ESV

[11] Yours, O LORD, is the greatness and the power and the glory and the victory and the majesty, for all that is in the heavens and in the earth is yours. Yours is the kingdom, O LORD, and you are exalted as head above all. [12] Both riches and honor come from you, and you rule over all. In your hand are power and might, and in your hand it is to make great and to give strength to all. [13] And now we thank you, our God, and praise your glorious name.

Psalm 150:1-6 ESV

[1] Praise the LORD! Praise God in his sanctuary; praise him in his mighty heavens! [2] Praise him for his mighty deeds; praise him according to his excellent greatness! [3] Praise him with trumpet sound; praise him with lute and harp!

Romans 11:33-36 ESV

[33] Oh, the depth of the riches and wisdom and knowledge of God! How unsearchable are his judgments and how inscrutable his ways! [34] "For who has known the mind of the Lord, or who has been his counselor?" [35] "Or who has given a gift to him that he might be repaid?" [36] For from him and through him and to him are all things. To him be glory forever. Amen.

Romans 16:25-27 ESV

[25] Now to him who is able to strengthen you according to my gospel and the preaching of Jesus Christ, according to the revelation of the mystery that was kept secret for long ages [26] but has now been disclosed and through the prophetic writings has been made known to all nations, according to the command of the eternal God, to bring about the obedience of faith- [27] to the only wise God be glory forevermore through Jesus Christ! Amen.

1 Timothy 1:17 ESV

[17] To the King of the ages, immortal, invisible, the only God, be honor and glory forever and ever. Amen.

Exodus 34:5-7 ESV

[5] The LORD descended in the cloud and stood with him there, and proclaimed the name of the LORD. [6] The LORD passed before him and proclaimed, "The LORD, the LORD, a God merciful and gracious, slow to anger, and abounding in steadfast love and faithfulness, [7] keeping steadfast love for thousands, forgiving iniquity and transgression and sin, but who will by no means clear the guilty, visiting the iniquity of the fathers on the children and the children's children, to the third and the fourth generation."

John 1:14 ESV

[14] And the Word became flesh and dwelt among us, and we have seen his glory, glory as of the only Son from the Father, full of grace and truth.

Psalm 8:1 ESV

O LORD, our Lord, how majestic is your name in all the earth! You have set your glory above the heavens.

Revelation 4:2-11 ESV

[2] At once I was in the Spirit, and behold, a throne stood in heaven, with one seated on the throne. [3] And he who sat there had the appearance of jasper and carnelian, and around the throne was a rainbow that had the appearance of an emerald. [4] Around the throne were twenty-four thrones, and seated on the thrones were twenty-four elders, clothed in white garments, with golden crowns on their heads. [5] From the throne came flashes of lightning, and rumblings and peals of thunder, and before the throne were burning seven torches of fire, which are the seven spirits of God, [6] and before the throne there was as it were a sea of glass, like crystal. And around the throne, on each side of the throne, are four living creatures, full of eyes in front and behind: [7] the first living creature like a lion, the second living creature like an ox, the third living creature with the face of a man, and the fourth living creature like an eagle in flight. [8] And the four living creatures, each of them with six wings, are full of eyes all around and within, and day and night they never cease to say, "Holy, holy, holy, is the Lord God Almighty, who was and is and is to come!" [9] And whenever the living creatures give glory and honor and thanks to him who is seated on the throne, who lives forever and ever, [10] the twenty-four elders fall

down before him who is seated on the throne and worship him who lives forever and ever. They cast their crowns before the throne, saying, [11] "Worthy are you, our Lord and God, to receive glory and honor and power, for you created all things, and by your will they existed and were created."

Isaiah 6:1-3 ESV

[1] In the year that King Uzziah died I saw the Lord sitting upon a throne, high and lifted up; and the train of his robe filled the temple. [2] Above him stood the seraphim. Each had six wings: with two he covered his face, and with two he covered his feet, and with two he flew. [3] And one called to another and said: "Holy, holy, holy is the LORD of hosts; the whole earth is full of his glory!"

Holy Communion

Communion is a way of celebrating and remembering the greatest act of love in history: Jesus giving his life for us on the cross. By taking the bread and the wine, we join in the New Covenant that Jesus established with his blood, making us part of his family forever (1 Corinthians 5:7). We also connect with the story of God's salvation plan, which was foretold by the prophets long before Jesus came to earth (Genesis 3:15, Psalm 22, Isaiah 53). Communion is not just a ritual, but a powerful reminder of the reality and the beauty of the gospel: Jesus died for our sins and rose again to give us eternal life.

1 Corinthians 11:23-32 AMP

[23] For I received from the Lord Himself that [instruction] which I passed on to you, that the Lord Jesus on the night in

which He was betrayed took bread; [24] and when He had given thanks, He broke it and said, "This is (represents) My body, which is [offered as a sacrifice] for you. Do this in [affectionate] remembrance of Me." [25] In the same way, after supper He took the cup, saying, "This cup is the new covenant [ratified and established] in My blood; do this, as often as you drink it, in [affectionate] remembrance of Me." [26] For every time you eat this bread and drink this cup, you are [symbolically] proclaiming [the fact of] the Lord's death until He comes [again]. [27] So then whoever eats the bread or drinks the cup of the Lord in a way that is unworthy [of Him] will be guilty of [profaning and sinning against] the body and blood of the Lord. [28] But a person must [prayerfully] examine himself [and his relationship to Christ], and only when he has done so should he eat of the bread and drink of the cup. [29] For anyone who eats and drinks [without solemn reverence and heartfelt gratitude for the sacrifice of Christ], eats and drinks a judgment on himself if he does not recognize the body [of Christ]. [30] That [careless and unworthy participation] is the reason why many among you are weak and sick, and a number sleep [in death]. [31] But if we evaluated and judged ourselves honestly [recognizing our shortcomings and correcting our behavior], we would not be judged. [32] But when we [fall short and] are judged by the Lord, we are disciplined [by undergoing His correction] so that we will not be condemned [to eternal punishment] along with the world.

Examine Yourself Before Communion

Communion is a sacred act that requires us to examine ourselves and repent of our sins before we partake of it. Verses 27-28 warn us not to take it in an unworthy manner, or we will be guilty of profaning the body and blood of the Lord. Verse 31 tells us how to avoid this: by judging ourselves and acknowledging our faults, for we have all sinned and fallen short of the glory of God. But we have hope in God's grace, as 1 John 1:8-9 ESV says: [8] "If we say we have no sin, we deceive ourselves, and the truth is not in us. [9] If we confess our sins, he is faithful and just to forgive us our sins and to cleanse us from all unrighteousness.

This confession must be sincere and accompanied by a change of heart and behavior. If our sin is unforgiveness, we should pray about it and ask God to help us discipline ourselves to forgive others as soon as we feel offended. Whatever temptations we face, our God is the solution, for

I can do all things through Christ who strengthens me. The Amplified says it this way: Philippians 4:13 AMP [13] I can do all things [which He has called me to do] through Him who strengthens and empowers me [to fulfill His purpose- I am self-sufficient in Christ's sufficiency; I am ready for anything and equal to anything through Him who infuses me with inner strength and confident peace.] Amen? Amen!

The Names of God

The Bible contains various names of God, each reflecting different aspects of His character and relationship with humanity. Here are some of the names and titles of God found in the Bible.

Our minds are too finite to comprehend God's infinite majesty and beauty in this life here on earth. But through the Bible, He gives us enough glimpses of His nature and deeds to encourage us to have faith and reverence for Him. I encourage you to occasionally incorporate these scripture-based names and attributes of God in your daily prayer and also as you worship Him. You'll be amazed by how much closer you feel to Him at the end.

These names are not just titles but represent the very nature of God and how He interacts with us. By studying these names, believers can gain deeper insight into who God is and how He desires to relate to us personally.

<u>The Lord Almighty</u>:

1 Samuel 17:45-46 NIV

[45] David said to the Philistine, "You come against me with sword and spear and javelin, but I come against you in the name of the Lord Almighty, the God of the armies of Israel, whom you have defied. [46] This day the Lord will deliver you into my hands, and I'll strike you down and cut off your head.

David invoked the Name of the Lord Almighty in this situation. How about you? Do you have any giants in your life that you would like to see destroyed? In the same way, in faith, call upon any of God's names or attributes in your prayers; He is the great I Am, and everything we need is found in Him, who loves us.

<u>Yahweh</u> is the most sacred name of God in the Hebrew Bible. It means "I am who I am" or "I will be who I will be." It expresses God's self-existence, sovereignty, and faithfulness to His promises.

Elohim: This is a plural name of God that implies His majesty, power, and creativity. It is often used in the context of God's creation of the world and His rule over all things.

Adonai: This is a name of God that means "Lord" or "Master". It shows God's authority, ownership, and lordship over His people and His creation.

El Shaddai: This is a name of God that means "God Almighty" or "God All-Sufficient". It reveals God's strength, sufficiency, and provision for His people.

Jehovah Jireh: This is a name of God that means "The Lord Will Provide". It was given by Abraham when God provided a ram as a substitute for Isaac on Mount Moriah (Genesis 22:14).

Jehovah Rapha: This is a name of God that means "The Lord Who Heals". It was given by Moses when God healed the bitter waters of Marah for the Israelites (Exodus 15:26).

Jehovah Nissi: This is a name of God that means "The Lord Is My Banner". It was given by Moses when God gave Israel victory over the Amalekites (Exodus 17:15).

Jehovah Shalom: This is a name of God that means "The Lord Is Peace". It was given by Gideon when God assured him of His presence and peace (Judges 6:24).

Jehovah Rohi: This is a name of God that means "The Lord Is My Shepherd". It is used by David in Psalm 23 to describe God's care, guidance, and protection for His sheep.

Jehovah Tsidkenu: This is a name of God that means "The Lord Is Our Righteousness." Jeremiah uses it to prophesy the coming of the righteous Branch, Christ (Jeremiah 23:6).

Jehovah Shammah: This is a name of God that means "The Lord Is There." Ezekiel uses it to describe the future glory of God's presence in the restored Jerusalem (Ezekiel 48:35).

Jesus: This is the name of the Son of God, who is also God incarnate. It means "Yahweh Saves" or "Yahweh Is Salvation". It shows that Jesus is the fulfillment of God's promise to save His people from their sins (Matthew 1:21).

Christ: This is Jesus's title, which means "Anointed One" or "Messiah." It shows that Jesus is the chosen and appointed King, Prophet, and Priest of God, who fulfills all the prophecies and promises of the Old Testament (John 1:41).

Immanuel: This is Jesus's name, which means "God With Us." It shows that Jesus is the manifestation of God's presence and love among His people (Matthew 1:23).

Alpha and Omega: These are the names of Jesus, which mean "The Beginning and the End". They show that Jesus is the eternal and sovereign Lord of all history and creation (Revelation 1:8).

The Word: This is a name of Jesus, which means "The Expression of God". It shows that Jesus is the perfect revelation of God's mind, will, and character (John 1:1).

The Lamb of God: This is a name of Jesus, which means "The Sacrifice of God". It shows that Jesus is the one who takes away the sin of the world by His death on the cross (John 1:29).

The Light of the World: This is a name of Jesus, which means "The Illumination of God". It shows that Jesus is the one who gives life, truth, and guidance to those who follow Him (John 8:12).

The Bread of Life: This is a name of Jesus, which means "The Sustenance of God". It shows that Jesus is the one who satisfies the hunger and thirst of the soul (John 6:35).

The Good Shepherd: This is a name of Jesus, which means "The Caretaker of God". It shows that Jesus is the one who loves, leads, and lays down His life for His sheep (John 10:11).

Attributes of God

The attributes of God in Christianity are qualities that define the nature and essence of God. They are often categorized into two main groups: infinite power and personality attributes. Here is a brief overview of the attributes.

Infinite Powers

<u>Omnipotence:</u> God's all-powerful nature, able to do anything that is in harmony with His character. Isaiah 55:11 [ESV] So shall my word be that goes out of my mouth; it shall not return to me empty, but it shall accomplish that which I sent it.

<u>Omniscient:</u> God's all-knowing nature, having complete knowledge of all things past, present, and future. 1 John 3:20 [ESV] For whenever our heart condemns us, God is greater than our heart, and He knows everything.

<u>Omnipresent:</u> God's presence everywhere at all times. Hebrews 4:13 [ESV] And no creature is hidden from his sight, but all are naked and exposed to the eyes of Him to whom we must give account.

<u>Eternity:</u> God's nature of being outside time, having no beginning or end. Romans 1:20 For His invisible attributes, namely, His eternal power and divine nature, have been clearly perceived, ever since the creation of the world, in the things that have been made. So they are without excuse.

<u>Immutability:</u> God's unchanging nature. And indivisible nature. Malachi 3:6 [ESV] For I the Lord do not change; therefore you, O children of Jacob, are not consumed.

<u>Sovereignty:</u> God's supreme power and authority over creation. Ephesians 1:11[ESV] In Him we have obtained an inheritance, having been predestined according to the counsel of His will.

Personality Attributes

<u>Holiness:</u> God's absolute purity and moral perfection. Ezekiel 38:23 [ESV] So I will show my greatness and my holiness and make myself known in the eyes of many nations. Then they will know that I am the Lord.

<u>Justice:</u> God's fairness and righteousness in dealing with His creation.

<u>Goodness:</u> God's benevolence and kindness towards creation.

<u>Love:</u> God's self-giving and sacrificial affection for His creation.

<u>Mercy:</u> God's compassion and forgiveness towards those who have erred.

<u>Grace:</u> God's unmerited favor and generosity.

<u>Truth:</u> God's reliability and faithfulness to His promises.

These attributes help believers understand God's character and form the basis of their relationship with Him. They are reflected in the Bible through God's interactions with humanity and are central to Christian theology.

My Closing Prayer for You.

Ephesians 3:14-19 ESV

[14] For this reason I bow my knees before the Father, [15] from whom every family in heaven and on earth is named, [16] that according to the riches of his glory he may grant you to be strengthened with power through his Spirit in your inner being, [17] so that Christ may dwell in your hearts through faith-that you, being rooted and grounded in love, [18] may have strength to comprehend with all the saints what is the breadth and length and height and depth, [19] and to know the love of Christ that surpasses knowledge, that you may be filled with all the fullness of God.

In Jesus' name, Amen.